The Secret Garden

Frances Hodgson Burnett

TEACHER GUIDE

NOTE:

The trade book edition of the novel used to prepare this guide is found in the Novel Units catalog and on the Novel Units website. Using other editions may have varied page references.

Please note: We have assigned Interest Levels based on our knowledge of the themes and ideas of the books included in the Novel Units sets, however, please assess the appropriateness of this novel or trade book for the age level and maturity of your students prior to reading with them. You know your students best!

ISBN 978-1-56137-062-7

opyright infringement is a violation of Federal Law.

2020 by Novel Units, Inc., St. Louis, MO. All rights reserved. No part of s publication may be reproduced, translated, stored in a retrieval system, or nsmitted in any way or by any means (electronic, mechanical, photocopying, cording, or otherwise) without prior written permission from Novel Units, Inc.

production of any part of this publication for an entire school or for a school tem, by for-profit institutions and tutoring centers, or for commercial sale is ictly prohibited.

vel Units is a registered trademark of Conn Education.

nted in the United States of America.

To order, contact your
local school supply store, or:

Toll-Free Fax: 877.716.7272
Phone: 888.650.4224
3901 Union Blvd., Suite 155
St. Louis, MO 63115

sales@novelunits.com

novelunits.com

Table of Contents

Summary 3

Introductory Activities 4

Twenty-Seven Chapters 9
    Chapters contain: Vocabulary Words,
    Discussion Questions, Predictions,
    Supplementary Activities

Culminating Activities 32

Background Information on Character
    for the Teacher 35

Vocabulary Activities 36

Map Activity 38

Assessment for *The Secret Garden* 39

Skills and Strategies

Writing
Journal, directions, advertisement, haiku

Literary Elements
Character, setting, plot development, dialect, conflict, direct and indirect characterization

Vocabulary
Synonyms/antonyms, context

Comprehension
Predicting, sequencing, cause/effect, inference, story mapping

Listening/Speaking
Participation in discussion and in dramatic activities

Thinking
Brainstorming, classifying and categorizing, evaluating, analyzing details

The Secret Garden   by Frances Hodgson Burnett

Summary

Mary Lennox, a sickly, lonely, orphan girl comes to live at her uncle's house. She finds the house and the servants mysterious and secretive. She meets Dickon, a servant's brother who opens up an interest in nature and the world around them. In the house Mary, discovers a lonely, unhappy invalid cousin. The three children learn a great deal about themselves and the world inside the Secret Garden.

Instructions Prior To Reading
Setting the Purpose

The following discussion questions and activities are designed to enhance your students' comprehension of the story by highlighting background experiences that are relevant to the reading. You may want to choose one or more of the activities, depending on which ones you think will best help your particular students understand and "own" the story as they read it.

Pre-Reading Discussion Questions

1. Lonely: Have you felt lonely, really lonely without a best friend or when your parents are gone or too busy? What was the situation? What did you do about it?

2. Friends: What does it take to make a friend or to be a friend? Have you ever noticed that sometimes a third person comes between two best friends? When have you seen this happen? Can it be prevented?

3. Anger: What do you do when you are angry with the whole world? How do you express it? Or do you? What are tantrums? If you were a parent, how would you handle a tantrum?

Recommended Procedure For Reading The Book

This book will be read one section at a time, using DRTA (Directed Reading Thinking Activity) Method. This technique involves reading a selection, predicting what will happen next (making good guesses) based on what has already occurred in the story. The children continue to read and everyone verifies the predictions.

The Secret Garden   by Frances Hodgson Burnett

Initiating Activity

1. Before we begin this novel, look at the front and back covers. Skim the Table of Contents. Read the first line of the story. Flip through the rest of the pages.

2. Based on the title, what do you think the story will be about?

3. Based on the chapter titles the author has chosen make a list of clues about the story. The teacher will list clues.

Prediction and Recommended Procedure Sheet

Using Predictions in the Novel Unit Approach:
We all make predictions as we read--little guesses about what will happen next, how the conflict will be resolved, which details given by the author will be important to the plot, details will help to fill in our sense of a character. Students should be encouraged to predict, to make sensible guesses. As students work on predictions, these discussion questions can be used to guide them: What are some of the ways to predict? What is the process of a sophisticated reader's thinking and predicting? What clues does an author give us to help us in making our predictions? Why are some predictions more likely than others?

A predicting chart is for students to record their predictions. As each subsequent chapter is discussed, you can review and correct previous predictions. This procedure serves to focus on predictions and to review the stories.

Predicting what will happen

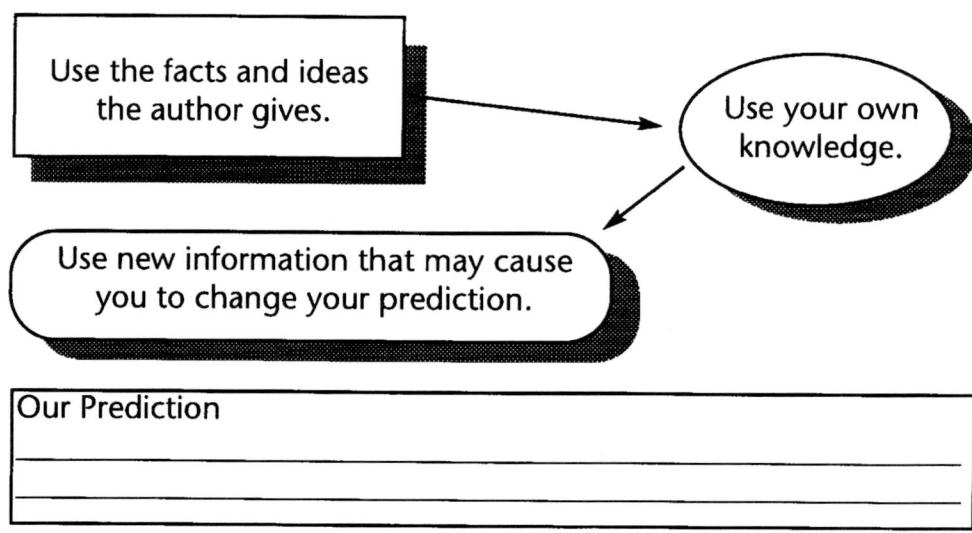

The Secret Garden   by Frances Hodgson Burnett

Prediction Chart

What Characters have we met so far?	What is the conflict in the story?	What are your predictions?	Why did you make those predictions?

The Secret Garden   by Frances Hodgson Burnett

Using Character Attribute Webs

Attribute webs are simply a visual representation of a character from the novel. They provide a systematic way for the students to organize and recap the information they have about a particular character. Attribute webs may be used after reading the novel to recapitulate information about a particular character or completed gradually as information unfolds, done individually, or finished as a group project.

One type of character attribute web uses these divisions:

> How a character acts and feels. (How does the character feel in this picture? How would you feel if this happened to you? How do you think the character feels?)
>
> How a character looks. (Close your eyes and picture the character. Describe him to me.)
>
> Where a character lives. (Where and when does the character live?)
>
> How others feel about the character. (How does another specific character feel about our character?)

In group discussion about the student attribute webs and specific characters, the teacher can ask for backup proof from the novel. You can also include inferential thinking.

Attribute webs may also be used to organize information about a concept or object or place.

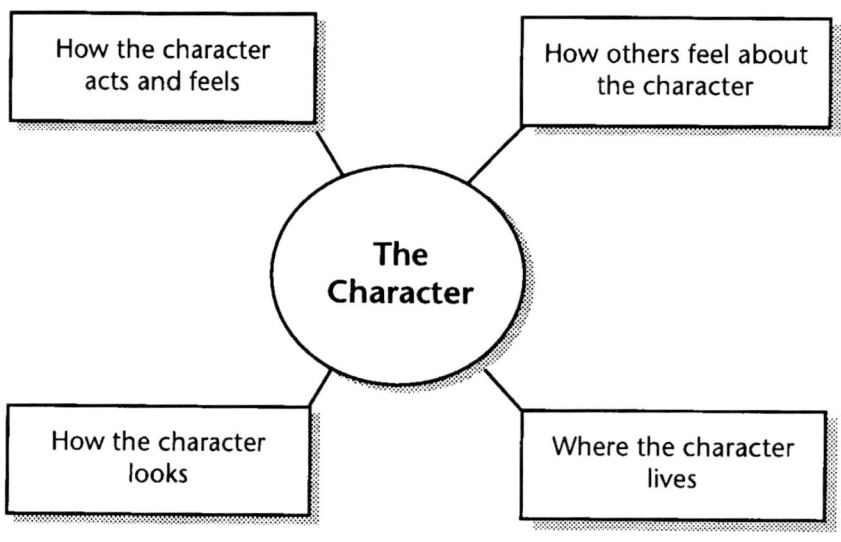

The Secret Garden — by Frances Hodgson Burnett

**Activity Sheet
for Attribute Webs**

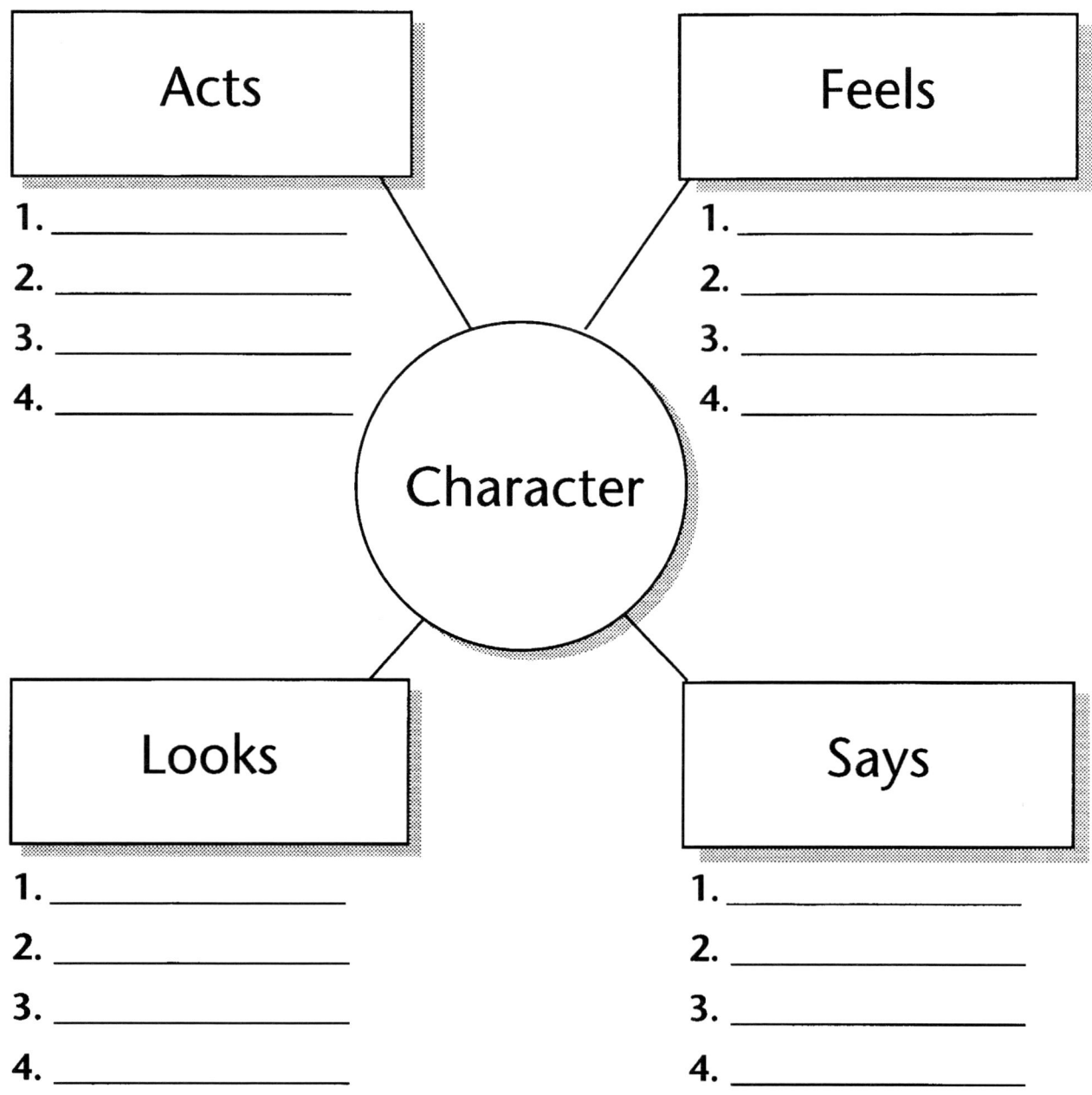

The Secret Garden by Frances Hodgson Burnett

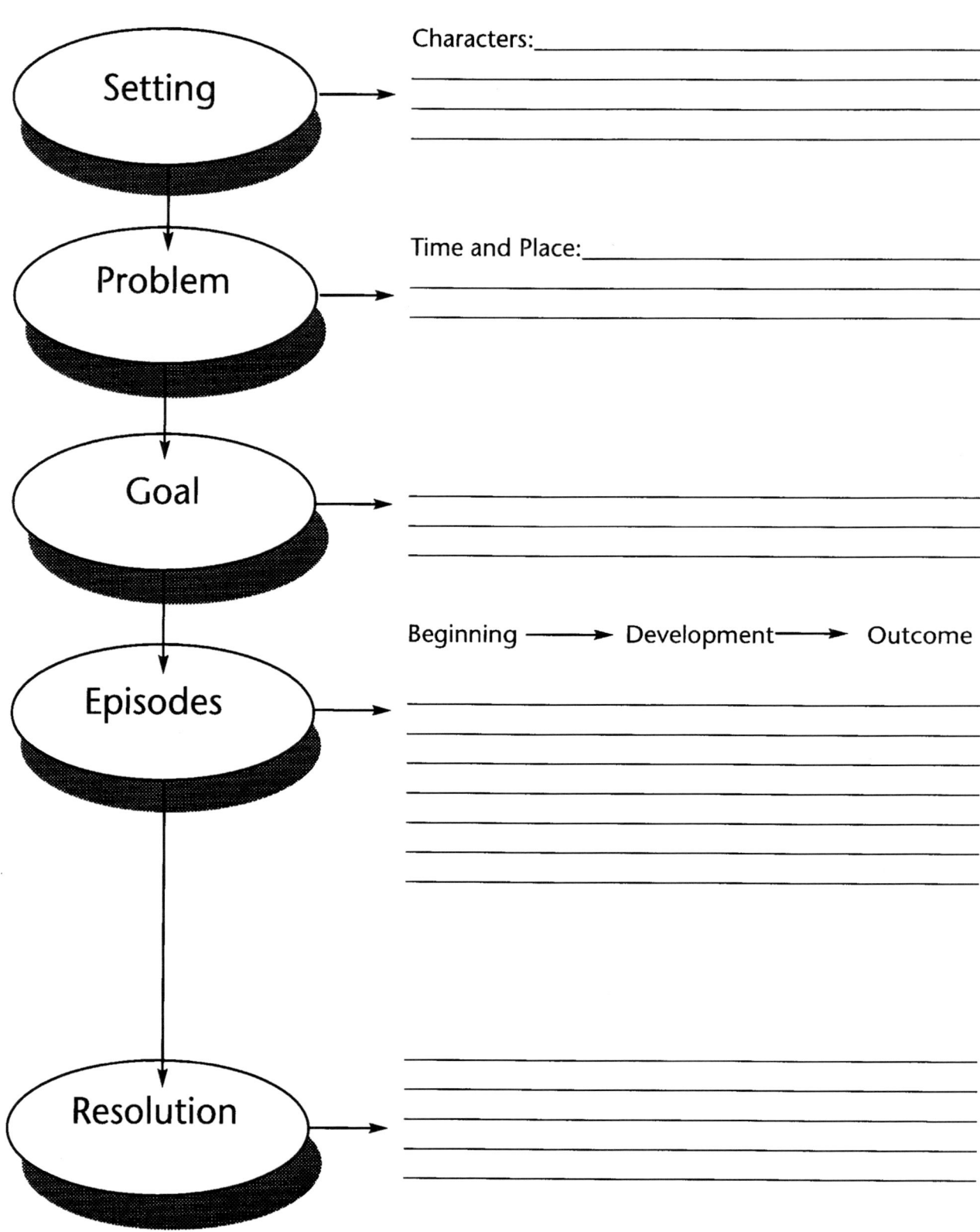

The Secret Garden
by Frances Hodgson Burnett

Chapter 1
There's No One Left
Pages 3 - 9

Vocabulary

fretful -p. 3
veranda -p. 5
disdaining -p. 5
wailing -p.6
cholera -p. 6
alternately -p. 6
drowsy -p.7
panic-stricken -p.7
bungalow -p.9

tyrannical -p. 4
hibiscus -p. 5
imploringly -p. 5
appalling -p.6
fatal -p.6
intensely -p.7
affectionate -p.7
desolation -p.8

1. Where had Mary been born? *India* Locate India and England on the map and the globe. The teacher explains that India was ruled by England for many years. (See map activity on page 38 of this guide.)

2. What are the duties of an Ayah? *p.1-2.* Would you want the job? Why or why not?

3. Why do you think Mary was such a dreadful child?

4. What is an orphan? Who usually cares for an orphan?

5. Brainstorm what life in India might have been like. What hints do you have in the first chapter that point to a very different life from yours?

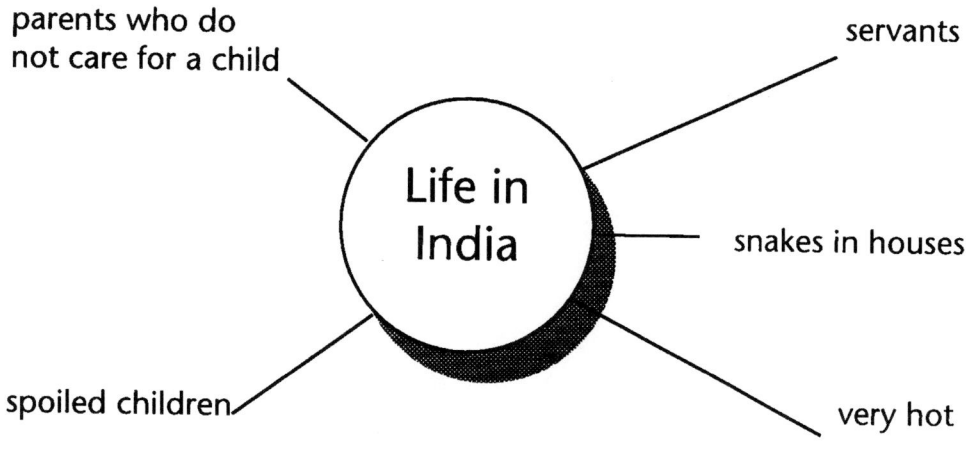

The Secret Garden   by Frances Hodgson Burnett

Research   Why did England rule India? How many years were the English in control of India?

Writing Activity Students will keep a journal of feelings, thoughts and questions about the story.

Social Studies   Develop a unit on the history, culture and geography of India.

Chapter 2
Mistress Mary
Quite Contrary
Pages 10-19

Vocabulary
untidy -p.11	furious -p.11
impudent -p.12	scorn -p.12
desolate -p.12	hunchback -p.12
horrid -p.12	sallow -p.14
alter -p.14	straggled -p.15
moor -p.16	

1. Mary is one of the main characters in the story. What is she like? Let us begin an attribute web of all the things we can learn about her. See Activity Sheet Attribute Web page 7.

2. How far is it from India to England? How long would it take to travel? Today how long would it take?

   Compare the house Mary was going to with your house. Use a T-diagram.

Your House	Mary's uncle's house in Yorkshire
	big house with 100 rooms
	servants
	gloomy
	gardens and a park
	sour uncle with a crooked back

© Novel Units, Inc.   All rights reserved

The Secret Garden
by Frances Hodgson Burnett

3. Make lists of words which describe Mary's feelings in this chapter. What is the best word? Compare with a classmate.

4. Begin a story map. Many stories have the same parts--a setting, characters, a problem, a series of events that lead to an ending or conclusion. These parts may be placed on a map or diagram that helps us to remember. Students may use the one included or make up one of their own. A large map may be displayed in the classroom. After each chapter is completed additions or changes to the map may be made.
   See Activity Sheet Story Map on page 12

   What information do we have to begin a story map?
   - Δ What is the setting (This changes from chapter 1 to 3)
   - Δ Who is the main character? (This may change or there may be more than one main character.)
   - Δ What is the problem?

Background Information on Character for the Teacher

The author may present his characters **directly** or **indirectly**. In direct presentation he tells us straight out what a character is like or has someone else in the story tell us what he is like.

In indirect presentation, the author shows us the character in action; we infer what he is like from what he thinks or says or does.

To be convincing, characterization, must also observe three other principles -- first, characters must be **consistent** in their behavior. They must not behave one way on one occasion and a different way on another unless there is a sufficient reason for change.

Second, characters must be clearly **motivated** in whatever they do, especially when there is any change in behavior.

Third, characters must be **plausible** or **lifelike**.

Change in character:
- Δ must be within the possibilities of character who makes it.
- Δ must be sufficiently motivated by circumstances in which character finds himself.
- Δ must be allowed sufficient time for change to believably take place.

The Secret Garden by Frances Hodgson Burnett

Activity Sheet
Story Map

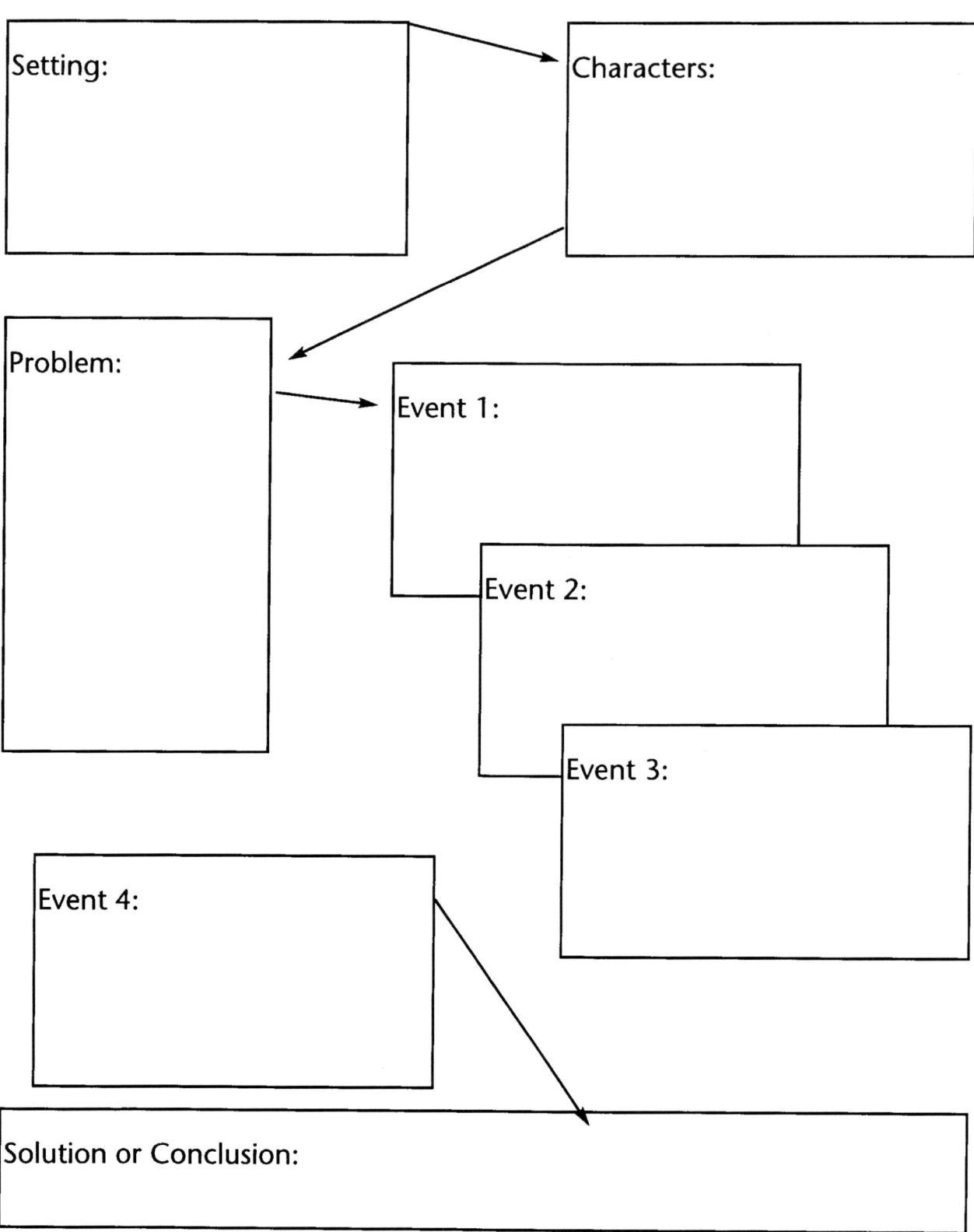

The Secret Garden   by Frances Hodgson Burnett

Chapter 3
Across the Moor
Pages 20-25

Vocabulary

waterproof -p. 20
brougham-p. 21
vicarage-p. 22
massive-p. 24

lulled-p. 20
burly-p. 21
immensely-p. 24
unceremoniously-p. 25

1. This story was first published in 1911 but the time of the story is even earlier. The setting of the story begins in India. Then Mary travels to England. Locate London in England and Yorkshire, on the classroom map.

Language Activity

2. Mary's language is much like ours but the servants in England speak a Yorkshire Dialect. A Dialect is passed on orally and reflects the vocabulary, usage and pronunciation of a particular region of a country or an ethnic origin or an occupation. Make a list of words in dialect that you are not sure of the meaning. We'll share these in class. Later some of these may be used in vocabulary games.

3. Compare the Sea with the Moor as Mary did. *p.23*
   Use the T Diagram.

Sea	Moor
Wind sounds like moor	miles of bushes and low plants
wild and dreary place	wind makes low rushing sound
black ocean	nothing lives on it except wild ponies and sheep
	dark moor

4. Do you think you would like Mary? Why or Why not?

5. How would you feel if your uncle would not even come to meet you?

Prediction

What will happen to Mary in her new home or would you even call it home?

The Secret Garden   by Frances Hodgson Burnett

Chapter 4
Martha
pages 26-44

Vocabulary

hearth-p. 26	tapestry-p. 26
turrets-p. 26	obsequious-p. 27
servile-p. 27	salaams-p. 27
haughtily-p. 28	indignantly-p. 29
vexed-p.29	unrestrainedly-p. 30
passionate-p. 30	subservient-p. 32
rustic-p.32	incredulously-p. 33
treacle-p. 33	victuals-p. 33
indignant-p.34	surly-p. 36

1. Introduce Vocabulary above using Vocabulary Activities 5 or 6 on page 36 of this guide.

2. How was Martha different form servants in India? *p.27 She talked to her mistress as an equal. Mary thought if she slapped Martha in the face that she might slap back.*

3. Why was Mary dressed in black? *Her parents had died.*

4. What did Mary mean when she said, "It was not the custom." *p.31 The native servants said this when someone told them to do a thing that their ancestors had not done for a thousand years.*

5. Why is one of the gardens locked? *p.35 It had been Mrs. Craven's garden. Mary wondered if Mr. Craven had liked his wife so much, why did he hate her garden. Do you have any ideas?*

6. How had the old gardener made friends with the robin? *He was too weak and couldn't fly back to the nest. The gardener had talked to him and probably fed him.*

7. Why did the old man call the robin the head gardener? *p.41 "He's always coming to see what I'm planting. He knows all the things Mr. Craven never troubled to find out."*

The Secret Garden
by Frances Hodgson Burnett

8. The teacher will make a Venn Diagram with the class comparing Ben Weatherstaff and Mary *p.42*

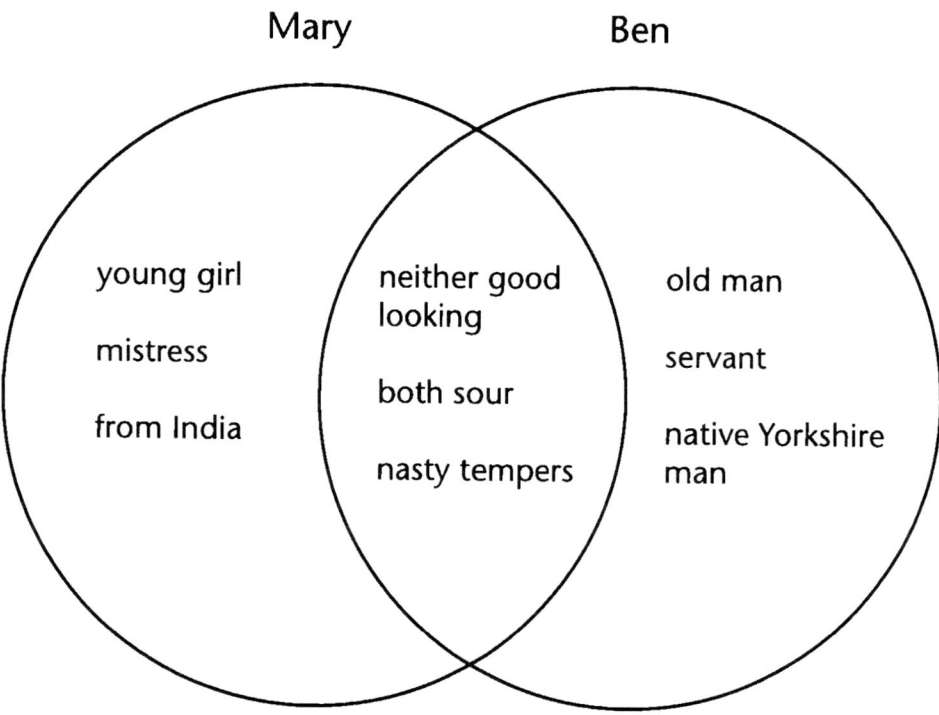

Prediction   Ben compares Mary's talking to the robin to Dickon's way with animals. What do you think will happen to Mary?

The Secret Garden   by Frances Hodgson Burnett

Chapter 5
The Cry in the Corridor
Pages 45 - 55

Vocabulary   porridge - p. 46   languid - p. 49
preen - p. 48   scullery-maid - p. 53

1. What happened in the garden that changed Mr. Craven's life? *p. 51 His wife fell off a tree branch seat and died.*

2. What were four good things that had happened to Mary? *p. 52*
   -- She understood the robin and the robin understood her
   -- She had run in the wind until her blood got warm
   -- She felt hungry for the first time
   -- She found out what it was to be sorry for someone.

3. Brainstorm the word **mystery**

   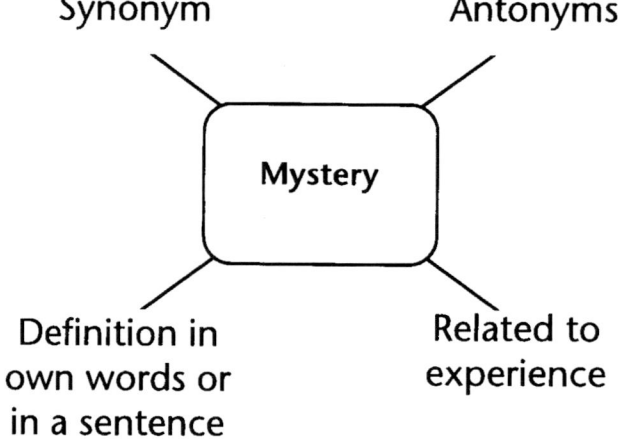

4. What noise did Mary think was mysterious? *p. 52 The wind sounded like a child crying.*

5. How did Mary know that Martha was not telling the truth? *p. 53 A door was opened and Mary heard a person. Martha acted troubled.*

6. How do we solve a mystery? What are some logical steps?
   -- Decide what you're looking for
   -- Question people
   -- Gather clues

Prediction   How will Mary solve the mystery?

The Secret Garden   by Frances Hodgson Burnett

Chapter 6
"There Was Someone Crying -- There Was"
Pages 54 - 62

Vocabulary   torrents - p. 54   bosom - p 55   resent - p. 55
                 perplexed - p. 55   inspired - p. 56   romping - p. 56
                 authority - p. 57   gallery - p. 58   mahouts - p. 59
                 palanquins - p. 59

1. Why do you think Mary liked stories about her mother and Dickon? *p. 55 She had really never known her mother and Dickon was interested in the outside animals like she was.*

2. How did Martha make Mary think very differently about getting dressed? *p. 57 She compared Mary to her four-year-old sister.*

3. What kind of live things did Mary find? *p. 60 mice.* How do you feel about mice?

4. Why did Mary like the carved elephant collection? What did she know about elephants? p. 59

Research   Elephants in India -- Kinds, Size, How they are used

Role-Play You are Mrs. Medlock and you have just caught Mary exploring the house, trying to find the mysterious crying.

Prediction Look at the next chapter title. What do you think will happen?

Chapter 7
The Key of the Garden
Pages 63 - 70

Activity 2 - See page 34 of this guide.

Vocabulary   reflective - p. 66   vixon - p. 66   indignantly - p. 67
                 wench - p. 68   contrary - p. 69   perennial - p. 69

1. Why did Mary think Dickon wouldn't like her? *p. 65 "Because no one does."* Why is this sad? *Because it is true.*

2. Who helped Mary find the key? *p. 69 the robin*

© Novel Units, Inc.   All rights reserved

The Secret Garden   by Frances Hodgson Burnett

Special Project   Look at the flower catalogs on the library table and in the encyclopedia. Can you find pictures of crocus, snowdrops and daffydowndillys?

Prediction   Is this the real key to the garden or could it be a magic key?

Special Project   How many of you have worked in a garden? In cooperative groups develop questions about gardening. Invite a person from a garden shop or nursery to answer the questions.

Special Project   Martha's family has 14 people. How many people are in your family? What is the grocery bill each week? How much money do your parents budget for food for each person in the family? Make a chart estimating what the grocery bill would be for 14 people. Would there be some items that you like that they could not afford?

Chapter 8
The Robin Who Showed the Way
Pages 71 - 81

Vocabulary   consult - p. 71   mystified - p. 75
                          impudence - p. 75   heathen - p. 78

1. Why is Mary changing?
   1. -- *with nothing to amuse her -- no toys, no one to pay attention to what she was doing, her imagination was awakening*

   2. -- *fresh air on the moor*

   3. -- *She was beginning to care and to want to do new things*

   4. -- *She had an appetite and began to feel less contrary*

2. Martha's brothers and sisters wanted to know about Mary. What stories did Mary promise to tell Martha? *p. 73-74 About riding on elephants and camels and going on tiger hunts.*

3. Who sent the jumping rope for Mary? *p. 75 Martha's mother.* How much did it cost? *tuppence.*

Research   How much is a tuppance worth in the United States today? Where could we find this information? How much does a jump rope cost in the U.S. today?

© Novel Units, Inc.   All rights reserved

The Secret Garden — by Frances Hodgson Burnett

4. How did Mary say, "Thank you!"? *p. 76 She shook Martha's hand.*

5. Do you believe in magic? Brainstorm the word **magic**.

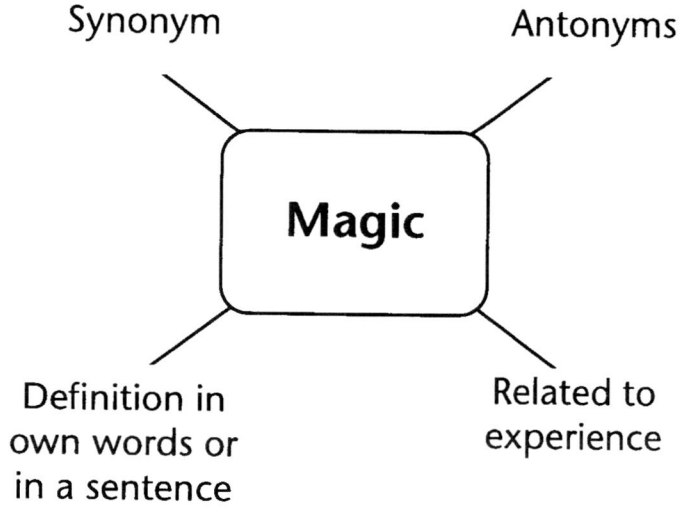

Prediction   What will Mary find in the secret garden?

Chapter 9
The Strangest House
Pages 82 - 93

Vocabulary   tendrils - 82   alcoves - p. 84
immensely - p. 85   pondered - p. 88

1. How did Mary learn about gardening? *p. 85 - 87 By digging, talking to Ben and Martha.*

2. Why did Mary want a spade? *p. 88* Why did she have to be careful? *She wanted to keep her garden a secret.*

3. Why did Martha and Mary write a letter? *p. 89 To ask Dickon to buy flower seeds and garden tools.*

4. Mary says Martha's mother doesn't seem to be like mothers in India. Do you have any ideas why there was a difference? Use a T-diagram to compare.

The Secret Garden   by Frances Hodgson Burnett

Mothers in India	Martha's Mother
-- servants do the work	-- is a servant
-- servants care for children	-- has many children
-- children do not really know their mothers	-- live in a small house
	-- do the housework
-- have few children	-- care for the children

5. Why does the house seem so strange to Mary? *p. 92 - 93 Martha will not admit there is someone crying in the house.*

Prediction   Who is crying? How will Mary investigate?

Chapter 10
Dickon
Pages 94 - 107

Vocabulary

intimate - p. 95   civil - p. 95   vain - p. 96
sarcastic - p. 97   engagingly - p. 97   ventured - p. 98
reluctantly - p. 99   flout - p. 105   obstinate - p. 107
imperious - p. 107

1. Why do you think Ben told Mary about the roses? Of whom did she remind him? *Mrs. Craven.*

2. How did Mary know Dickon? *p. 101 Because he could charm the rabbits and pheasants like the natives charmed snakes in India.*

3. Why was Mary afraid to tell Dickon about her garden? *p. 106 She wonders if he'll keep it secret.*

Prediction   How will Dickon help Mary with the secret garden? Did she choose a good person with whom to share a secret? Why or why not?

The Secret Garden   by Frances Hodgson Burnett

Chapter 11
The Nest of
Missel Thrush
Pages 108-117
Vocabulary

reverent - p. 109   wick - p. 110   exultantly - p. 110
industriously - p. 111   mournfully - p. 116   distended - p. 117

1. How did Dickon help Mary? *p. 110 Showed her how to tell the dead wood from the live; praised her hard work.*

2. Dickon thinks someone besides the robin had been in the garden since it was shut 10 years ago. Who could have pruned? *p. 114*

3. Who does Mary like? *Dickon, his mother, Martha, Ben and the robin.*

4. How does the author make Dickon seem different from the other characters? He almost seems too good. Make an attribute web for Dickon. Add to it after reading each chapter.

Prediction   Will someone or something spoil the secret garden?

Chapter 12
"Might I Have a
Bit of Earth"
Pages 118 - 128

Vocabulary:

exultantly - p. 118   obstinately - p. 119   brooch - p. 121
fretted - p. 122   rouse - p. 123   tremulously - p. 124
wretched - p. 124   woefully - p. 127

1. Why did Mr. Craven want to see Mary? *p. 123 Martha's mother had talked to him.*

2. What did Mr. Craven learn about Mary? *p. 123 - 125*
   -- she was very thin
   -- she did not want a nurse or governess
   -- she wanted to play outdoors
   -- she wanted a bit of earth to plant seeds
   -- she wanted to visit Martha's mother

3. Of whom did Mary remind Mr. Craven? *p. 125 Mrs. Craven.* In what ways?

The Secret Garden   by Frances Hodgson Burnett

Prediction   This a long book. What other adventures could a little orphan girl have?

Look at the chapter title. Chapter titles give clues. Who do you think Colin will be?

Chapter 13
I Am Colin
Pages 128 - 143

Vocabulary   rebellious - p. 129   mystified - p. 132
                          peculiar - p. 137   persistently - p. 138

1. What secret message did Mary see in Dickon's picture?
   p. 128 Mary's garden was her nest and she was like the missel thrush.

2. Mary decided to find whoever was crying. Would you be brave enough to wander around in a house with 100 rooms with only a candle?

3. Make an attribute web to describe Colin.
   Possible answers:
           sharp delicate face
           eyes too big -- agate gray
           heavy hair
           stays in his room because he gets tired
           might become a hunchback
           hates fresh air
           curious
           spoiled
           cross
           10 years old
           queer in some ways

4. How did Mary convince him to keep the garden a secret?
   p. 139 What characteristics can we add to Mary's web?
   kind and clever.

The Secret Garden by Frances Hodgson Burnett

Chapter 14
A Young Rajah
Pages 144 - 157

Vocabulary rajah - p. 144   vexes - p. 145   tantrums - p. 145
agitated - p. 146   bewitched - p. 146   raved - p. 147
reproachfully - 155

1. Why was Martha frightened when she learned Mary had talked to Colin? *p. 145 She was afraid she'd get into trouble and lose her job.*

2. Martha thought Mary bewitched Colin. Why do you think Colin didn't continue his tantrum? What would you have done with him?

3. What two things did Mary tell Colin? *p. 150*
   -- about a boy in India who spoke to servants like Colin did
   -- how different Colin was from Dickon.

4. What was the doctor's advice to Colin? *p. 156*
   -- Don't talk too much
   -- Don't forget you are sick
   -- Don't forget you get tired

5. Why was Mary better than medicine for Colin? *p. 154*
   -- She told interesting stories
   -- She made him laugh
   -- She got him to eat

Answers to p. 24   Colin   Alike   Mary

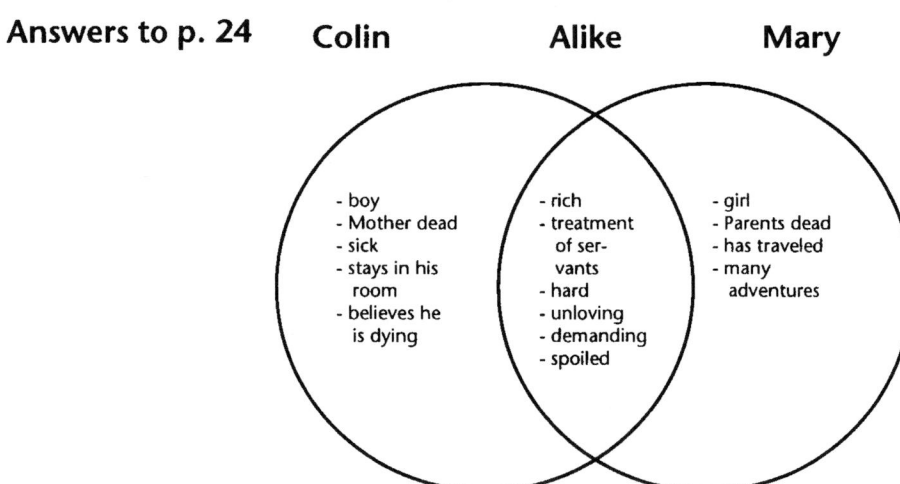

- boy
- Mother dead
- sick
- stays in his room
- believes he is dying

- rich
- treatment of servants
- hard
- unloving
- demanding
- spoiled

- girl
- Parents dead
- has traveled
- many adventures

The Secret Garden by Frances Hodgson Burnett

Activity Sheet

6. How are Colin and Mary alike?

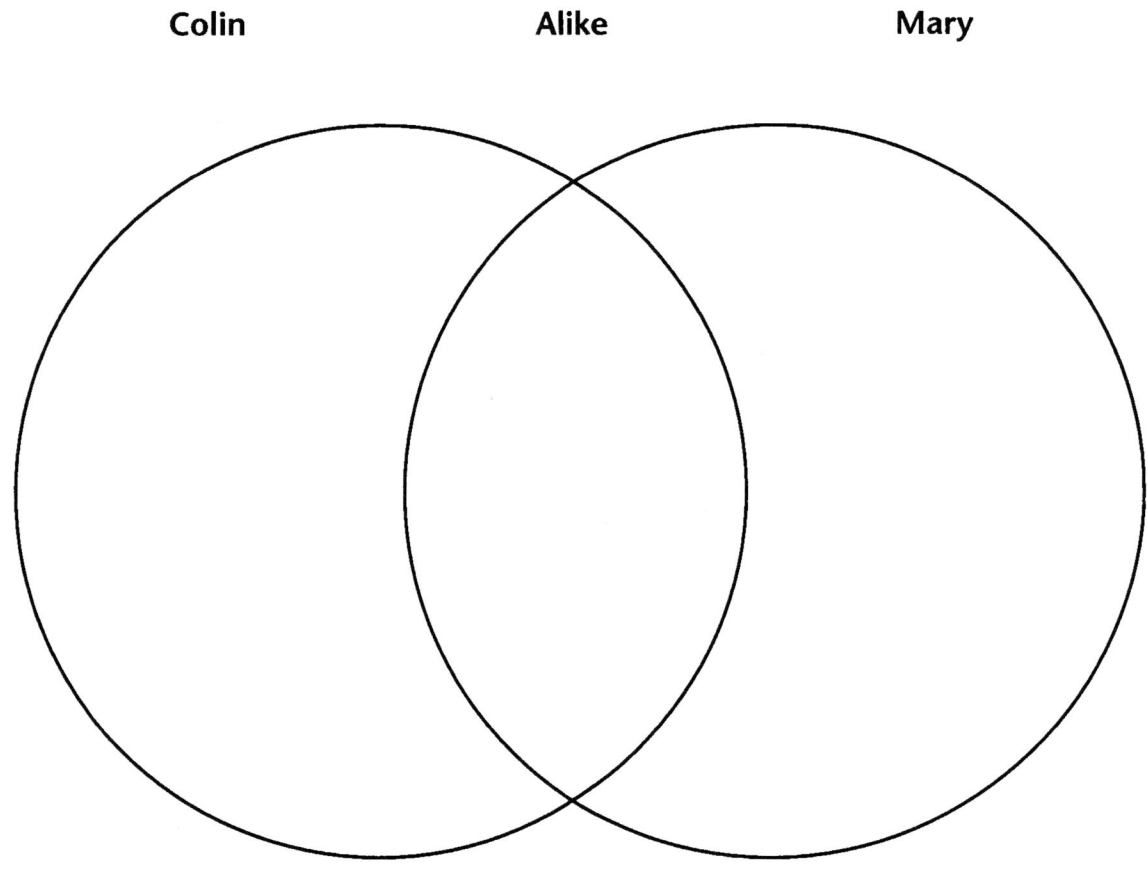

Colin   Alike   Mary

The Secret Garden   by Frances Hodgson Burnett

Chapter 15
Nest Building
Pages 158 - 172

1. Why did Colin think he'd like Dickon? *p. 161 He was an animal charmer.*

2. How did Mary feel some magic had been worked in the world? *p. 162 Spring had come to the garden.*

3. Dickon speaks English but he uses a Yorkshire dialect. How would you say, "...Ben Weatherstuff's robin will stay here if us don't flight him"?

Chapter 16
""I Won't."
Said Mary.
Pages 173 - 181

Vocabulary

rook - p. 174   doleful - p. 175   condescended - p. 176
retorted - p. 177   pathetic - p. 177   hysterics - p. 179
unrelenting - p. 179

1. Why did Colin and Mary fight? *p. 176 Mary worked in the garden with Dickon instead of talking to Colin.* Do you think it is harder for three people to be friends rather than two? Why or why not?

2. Why did the nurse laugh at the fight? *p. 178 She thought it was funny for someone to stand up to Colin.*

3. Colin and Mary had an argument -- a conflict. There are three main types of conflict: 1) a person against a person; 2) person against nature or society; 3) person against himself or herself. Which type of conflict was this? Watch closely for more conflicts in this novel.

Prediction   Will Mary ever go back to talk to Colin? Why or why not?

Chapter 17
A Tantrum
Pages 182 - 190

Vocabulary   restrain - p. 184   contradict - p. 184   writhe - p. 185
ventured - p. 187

© Novel Units, Inc.   All rights reserved

The Secret Garden   by Frances Hodgson Burnett

1. Why would the nurse ask Mary to help stop Colin's tantrum?

2. Why did Mary say such awful things to Colin? *p. 184 She was angry.*

Role Play   Mary stopping the tantrum.

3. Why did the nurse show Mary Colin's back? *p. 186 Colin told her to. He wanted to prove there was a lump.*

Chapter 18
"Tha Munnot Waste No Time"
Pages 191 - 198

Vocabulary   modify - p. 193

1. What did Martha's mother say are the two worst things that can happen to a child? *p. 191*
   -- *never to have his own way*
   -- *always to have his own way*
   What do you think she meant? Give some examples.

2. Why must Mary not talk Yorkshire dialect to Colin? *Yorkshire dialect was spoken by the servants or lower classes.*

3. How are Mary, Colin, and Ben Weatherstaff alike? *p. 196*
   -- *not much to look at*
   -- *sour as they looked*
   -- *bad tempers*

4. Why do you think Mary told Colin about the door?

Chapter 19
"It Has Come."
Pages 199 - 212

Vocabulary
unscrupulous - p. 201   bromide - p. 202   volubly - p. 203
waft - p. 205   recluse - p. 207   austerely - p. 208
overwhelmed - p. 209   ravenous - p. 210 ecstasy - p. 210
excursions - p. 210

1. Why didn't Dr. Cravin want Colin to get well? *p. 201 He would lose all chance of inheriting the estate.*

The Secret Garden   by Frances Hodgson Burnett

2. How is Colin like a Rajah? What is a **Rajah?** *a prince, chief or ruler in India.* Make a T-comparison.

Colin	Rajah
Actions: -- lives in England -- rules the servants **Speech:** -- gives orders to the servants -- haugty -- bossy **Dress:** -- rich robes	-- lives in India -- ruler -- gives orders -- rich robes -- wear ruby rings

3. Why had Colin never talked to a boy in his life? *p. 209 He had been an invalid and a recluse.*

4. What did Colin and Dickon talk about? Why were they very different boys? *Colin had been sick and protected and he was rich. Dickon was a poor boy with many brothers and sisters. He had been free to roam outside.*

Prediction   Will Colin be disappointed when he sees the garden?

Chapter 20
"I Shall Live Forever."
Pages 213 - 223

Vocabulary
intimate - p. 213   rational - p. 214   elaborately - p. 214
uncanny - p. 215   menagerie - p. 215   leniently - p. 215
impudence - p. 215   trample - p. 217   morbid - p. 218

1. Why did Colin give such strange orders to Mr. Roach? *p. 216 He wanted to go outside to the secret garden without anybody but Colin and Mary knowing.*

2. What does Mrs. Medley mean when she says, "If he does live and that Indian child stays here, I'll warrant she teaches him that the whole orange does not belong to him?" *p. 217 Mary will teach Colin to share and probably have some fights with him.*

Prediction   Who will be the next person to learn about the secret garden?

The Secret Garden   by Frances Hodgson Burnett

Chapter 21
Ben Weatherstaff
Pages 224 - 235

Vocabulary

immense - p. 224	radiantly - p. 225	crumpets - p. 229
cautious - p. 230	harangued - p. 231	obstinately - p. 232
torrent - p. 232	imperiously - p. 232	haughtily - p. 233
gnarled - p. 233	tactless - p. 233	falter - p. 235

1. What made the afternoon in the garden so special?

2. Who discovered the children in the secret garden? *p. 231 Ben*

Chapter 22
When the Sun Went Down
Pages 236 - 243

Vocabulary

testily - p. 237	exultation - p 238
crabbed - p. 238	obstinacy - p. 240

1. If Mary didn't work magic, how did Colin stand up, walk, and plant the rose? *p. 237 - 241 Mary encouraged Colin, but it wasn't magic. It was positive thinking.*

2. Why do Colin and Ben get along? *Colin looks like his mother and Weatherstaff liked her.*

3. Why is the chapter titled, "When the Sun Went Down?" *p. 243 Colin said, "And the sun is slipping over the edge... I want to be standing when it goes. That's part of the magic."*

© Novel Units, Inc.   All rights reserved

The Secret Garden   by Frances Hodgson Burnett

Chapter 23
Magic
Pages 244 - 257

Vocabulary

prejudice - p. 245	defying - p. 247	fakirs - p. 250
imposing - p. 250	majestic - p. 253	enraptured - p. 253
dervishes - p. 253	solemnity - p. 255	morbid - p. 257

1. How did Mary tell Colin that being rude was not the way to act? *p. 245 "Nobody ever dared to do anything you didn't like -- because you were going to die.*

2. How are Ben Weatherstaff, Mary, and Colin alike? *They are a bit queer, act differently from other people and have not had the civilizing effect of a family or living with other people.*

3. What's the difference between white magic and black magic? *p. 246 White magic is good magic -- all the happy times in the garden. Black magic is evil, and unhappy and scary.*

4. What did Colin mean when he said, "I am sure there is Magic in everything, only we have not sense enough to get hold ot if and make it do things for us...?" Give some examples.

5. What is the big secret, the Magic that Colin is going to work on in the garden? *p. 256 He is going to learn to walk and run like every other boy.*

Chapter 24
"Let Them Laugh."
Pages 258 - 272

Vocabulary

domain - p. 260	revelation - p. 262	bounteous - p. 267
grandeur - p. 267	copious draughts - p. 267	intervals - p. 268
gentry - p. 269	repress - p. 271	

1. Why does Colin continue his groaning and fretting? *p. 261 The servants would think something was wrong if he changed.*

2. Why were Colin and Mary planning "play action"? *p. 264 They did not want the doctor or nurse to write to Mr. Craven.*

© Novel Units, Inc.   All rights reserved

The Secret Garden   by Frances Hodgson Burnett

    3. How did Dickon help Colin get in shape? *p. 269 He talked to an athlete and learned about exercises to help Colin.*

    4. How and why did the children trick the nurse and doctor about eating? *p. 270 Mrs. Sowerby was sending food. The children were not eating all the food the cook prepared.*

Extra   Develop an exercise program for Colin. Write directions and make charts of how to do the exercises.

Chapter 25
The Curtain
Pages 273 - 280

Vocabulary   conveyed - p. 273   disconcerting - p. 275
restive - p. 276   inordinately - p. 277

    1. Colin and Mary took advantage of the rainy days by exploring the house. What would you do in a mysterious house with 100 rooms on a rainy day?

    2. Why did Colin cover his mother's picture? Why in this chapter did he uncover it? *p. 280 It had made Colin angry to see his mother's laughing face, but with Magic all around, Colin wanted to see the picture.*

Prediction   What will Mr. Craven think of the new Colin? Remember Mr. Craven was not a happy person either.

Chapter 26
"It's Mother."
Pages 281 - 292

Vocabulary   incantations - p. 281   rapturous - p. 284   tremulously - p. 288

    1. Why do you think Ben cried when the children sang the Doxology? *p. 286 "I never seed no sense in the Doxology before."*

    2. Why had Mr. Craven ignored or paid no attention to his son? *p. 301 Because Mrs. Craven had died.*

    3. Why do you think Dickon is a very special person? In this chapter the reader sees how special Dickon's mother is.

The Secret Garden   by Frances Hodgson Burnett

Prediction   How will Colin greet and meet his father?

Chapter 27
In the Garden
Pages 293 - 311

Vocabulary   hypochondriac - p. 294   hideous - p. 294   vaguely - p 298
                   salver - p. 299   bloat - p. 304   suppressed - p. 305

1. What was Colin's scientific experiment? *p. 294 to think beautiful thoughts is the way to become healthy.*

2. Why did Mr. Craven begin to change? *p. 296 He began to really see the beautiful flowers in a mountain valley. He began to feel really alive.*

3. Why did Mr. Craven decide to go home? *p. 299 He had a dream and he received a letter from Susan Sowerby.*

4. Why was it the wrong Magic for Mr. Craven to say, "Too late"? *White Magic is positive thinking.*

5. How was Colin's meeting with his father different than he planned? *p. 307 Colin was running a race and almost ran into his father's arms.*

The Secret Garden   by Frances Hodgson Burnett

Culminating Activities:

1. Complete the story map.

2. Briefly describe the setting, or time and place, with which the story begins.

3. Describe the main problem.

4. Summarize at least three key events in the story.

5. Tell what the climax was. In other words, where was the point of greatest tension, where you knew the problem couldn't get any worse?

6. Describe the resolution, or what happened after the climax until the end of the story.

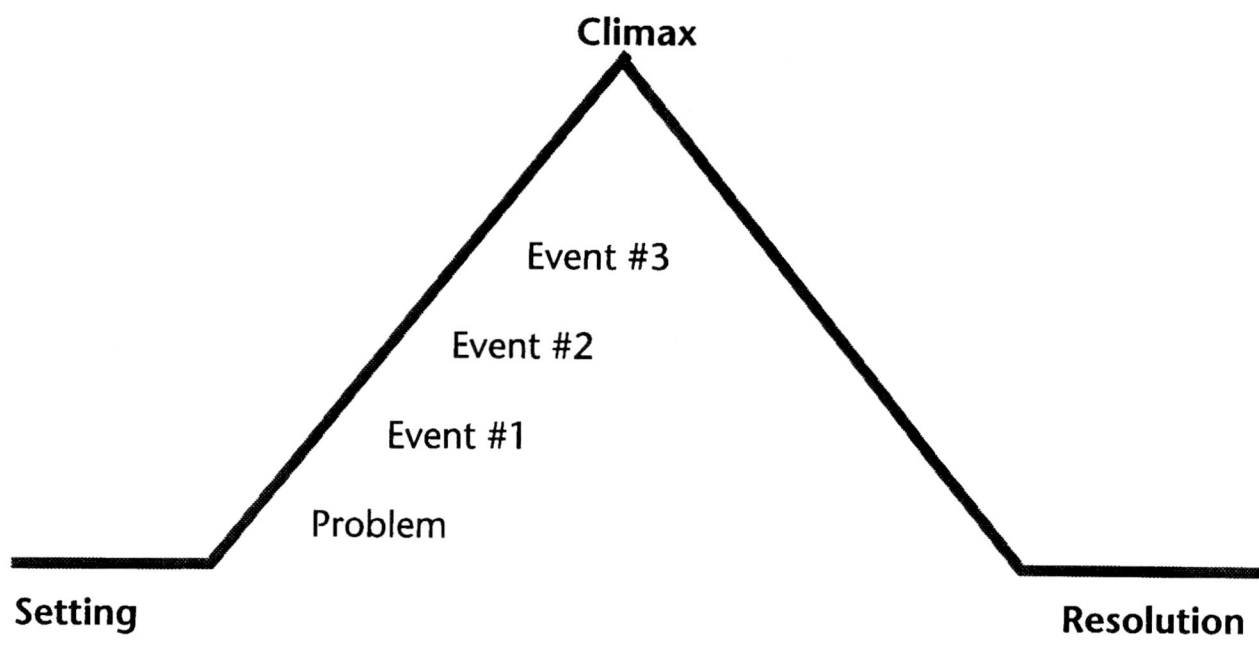

The Secret Garden   by Frances Hodgson Burnett

2. Sociogram   Think about the relationships each of the main characters has with the others. Complete the following "sociogram." First place the character names in the circles (with the main character in the center circle). Then label each arrow with a word or phrase that tells what one person does to another (or how one person feels about another.) Then label each arrow with a word or phrase that tells what one person does to another (or how one person feels about another.) Then label each arrow with a word or phrase that tells what one person does to another (or how one person feels about another.) For example, the arrow between Dicken and Colin might be labeled, "distrusts and feels sorry for."
(see activity sheet p.34)

3. Create a poster to advertise the story so people will want to read it.

4. Watch a video tape of the *Secret Garden*. Fill in a comparison/contrast chart using a T-Diagram.

5. Decide which character in the story you would like to spend a day with. Draw a picture of this character and write why you'd like this person.

6. Decide if this story really could have happpened.

7. Write a Haiku poem about the *Secret Garden* or any of the characters. A Haiku poem is a 3 line unrhymed verse with 5, 7, and 5 syllables respectively. Display these poems on a Bulletin Board with words *Secret Garden*. Students may draw pictures of flowers or may cut out pictures from garden catalogs to make collages.

The Secret Garden by Frances Hodgson Burnett

Activity Sheet

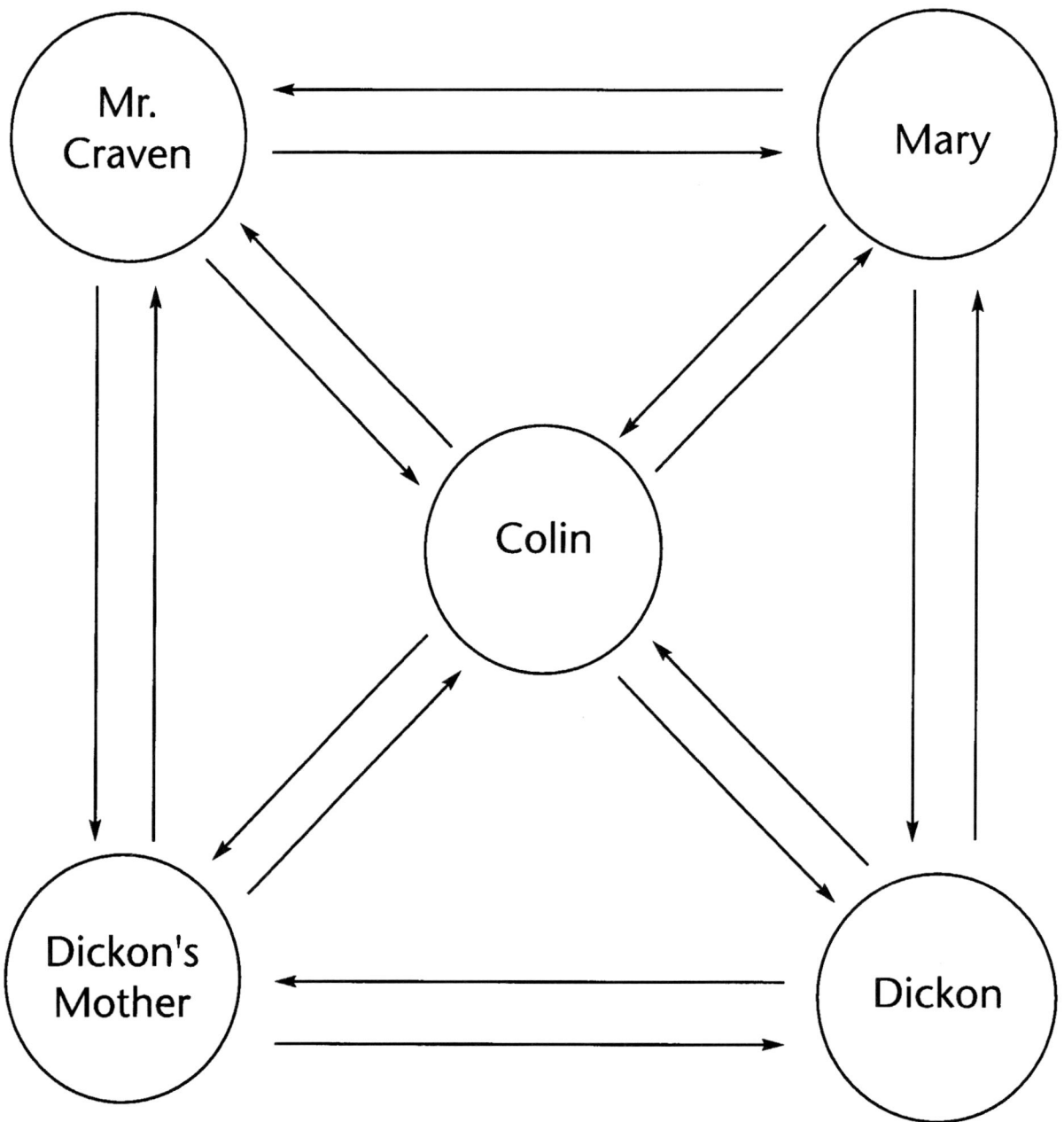

The Secret Garden
by Frances Hodgson Burnett

Background Information On Character For The Teacher

The author may present his characters **directly** or **indirectly**. In direct presentation he tells us straight out what a character is like or has someone else in the story tell us what he is like.

In indirect presentation, the author shows us the character in action; we infer what he is like from what he thinks or says or does.

To be convincing, characterization, must also observe three other principles -- first, characters must be **consistent** in their behavior. They must not behave one way on one occasion and a different way on another unless there is a sufficient reason for change.

Second, characters must be clearly **motivated** in whatever they do, especially when there is any change in behavior.

Third, characters must be **plausible** or **lifelike**.

Change in character:

- Δ must be within the possibilities of character who makes it.
- Δ must be sufficiently motivated by circumstances in which character finds himself.
- Δ must be allowed sufficient time for change to believably take place.

The Secret Garden — by Frances Hodgson Burnett

Vocabulary Activities

1. Develop word maps. Use color to distinguish antonyms, synonyms, etc.

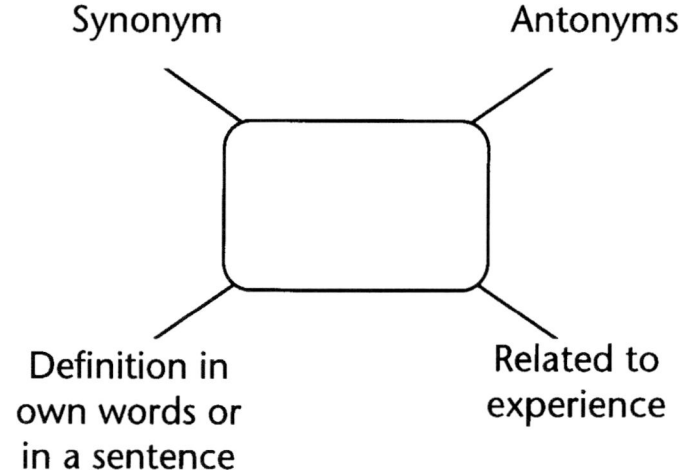

2. Crossword Puzzles--Have students use vocabulary words from the chapter to make crossword puzzles on graph paper. They should write a question for each word and develop an answer sheet. The teacher will check and then distribute the puzzles to other students to work out in their free time.

3. One student picks a word from the vocabulary list or cards. Another student has ten (or five) questions to discover the word and give the definition.

4. List vocabulary words on large sheets of paper. Leave space for students to a) illustrate the meaning next to each word; b) list a memory device to remember the word.

5. List the vocabulary words on the board or on a sheet of paper in the form of a table. Pronounce the words. Ask the students to rate their knowledge of each of the words (as a group, in cooperative groups or individually.)

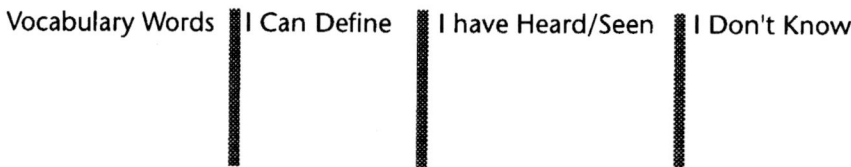

6. Provide vocabulary challenge words in context. Ask students to "guess" at the meaning form context, asking why for each guess. Generate a listing of the "why answers" to teach context clues.

The Secret Garden   by Frances Hodgson Burnett

7. Select ten words. Write only every other letter and a synonym or definition. Exchange student papers. Example: a_o_a: (aroma).

8. Word Sort:
    I can say
    I know what it means
    I do not know

9. Word Sort:
    Action
    Things
    Places
    Names

10. I am thinking of a word that:
    has a long sound
    begins with the same sound as Pat
    means _____
    is a synonym of

11. Divide the vocabulary words among pairs of students. Have the student pairs act out their word while the class guesses which word is being portrayed.

12. Have the students play "Win, Lose, or Draw" with the vocabulary words (after they have met the words in context). Two three-person teams play against each other. One person draws a card containing a vocabulary word and is given one minute to draw clues on a sketch pad to elicit the word—plus its definition—from teammates. (The drawing might be a representation of the concept, or a rebus that clues teammates in to the word's sounds.) The team with the total number of correct guesses after all time is up wins.

13. Make a vocabulary activity for a classmate. Use more than the vocabulary from just one chapter. Pick five words and write synonyms. Arrange the words and synonyms so they may be matched. Write an answer key.

The Secret Garden   by Frances Hodgson Burnett

Map Activity

1. Mark India with an I.

2. Mark England with an E.

3. Mark the United States with a U.

4. How many miles is it from India to England? How fast did ships go in the late 1800s? How long would it take for Mary to travel to England?

5. How many miles is it from New York City to England?

6. How many miles is it from India to New York City?

7. How long would it take to fly to England from New York City?

8. How long would it take to fly to India from New York City?

The Secret Garden   by Frances Hodgson Burnett

Assessment for *The Secret Garden*

Assessment is an on-going process, more than a quiz at the end of the book. Points may be added to show the level of achievement. When an item is completed, the teacher and the student check it.

Name _____ Date _____

Student   **Teacher**

_____   _____   1. Keep a reaction journal for each chapter of the novel.

_____   _____   2. Make an attribute web for one of the characters in the novel. (See pages 6-7 of this guide.)

_____   _____   3. Create a collage to represent important ideas of the book.

_____   _____   4. Complete one of the suggested research projects—history, culture, geography of India, English rule of India, elephants in India, names and value of English money. Use graphic organizers and present your findings to a small group of classmates.

_____   _____   5. Make a list of words in Yorkshire dialect.

_____   _____   6. Create a poster to advertise the story of *The Secret Garden*.

_____   _____   7. Decide which character in the story you would like to spend a day with. Draw a picture of this character and write why you like this person.

_____   _____   8. With a classmate role play one incident in the story.

_____   _____   9. Divide a sheet of paper in four sections. What are the four most important parts of this story? Draw an illustration of each of these important parts.

_____   _____   10. Write a self-assessment about your work, behavior, and effort on this unit.

© Novel Units, Inc.   All rights reserved